T0145187

ROAD TRIPPING FROM ALASKA TO NEW YORK CITY

JOURNALING THE JOURNEY AND TAKING PIX ALONG THE WAY

Sharon R. Leippi

Balboa Press books may be ordered through booksellers or by contacting:

Balboa Press
A Division of Hay House
1663 Liberty Drive
Bloomington, IN 47403
www.balboapress.com
1 (877) 407-4847

ISBN: 978-1-5043-9294-5 (sc)
ISBN: 978-1-5043-9295-2 (e)

Library of Congress Control Number: 2017918026

Print information available on the last page.

Balboa Press rev. date: 07/11/2019

BALBOA
PRESS
A DIVISION OF HAY HOUSE

BEFORE THE JOURNEY

Three weeks before the journey – checked with the veterinarian and got a clean bill of health for Chopper, my prized feline friend and traveling companion.

Two weeks before the journey – new tires, new brakes, and an oil change for my 2004 Ford Explorer.

Ten days before the journey – purchased a kennel for Chopper, and made up several disposable litter boxes for the kennel and for motels.

One week before the journey – dropped off a box of fourteen Fire & Ice cookbooks for the bookseller at Anchorage's airport, and checked with the museum.

Five days before the journey – left Anchorage at nine in the morning and drove to Whittier with a friend Yvonne for a day cruise, to experience glaciers and wildlife.

Three days before the journey – filled three gallon jugs with distilled water.

Two days before the journey – considered the option of calling my telephone company to request a passport calling plan because I wanted to place calls from Canada.

One day before the journey – checked with auto insurance agent, who gave me a road atlas, about purchasing towing insurance for driving in Canada.

The day of the journey – packed the SUV including snacks:

- dried fruit
- nuts
- bottled juices
- apples
- cans of tuna for Chopper

I grabbed my sunglasses and then Chopper and I left Anchorage in the late afternoon of the last week of May for our road trip.

Day 1 – Starting the Journey from Alaska

I loaded Chopper into his kennel cage and it was about five p.m. when we left Anchorage for New York City. There was still a lot of driving time, as the sun was setting at midnight and rising about four a.m.

We drove past Palmer, and then when I noticed that radio reception was dimming I just turned the radio off. Chopper's cat toys (birds and cricket) started chirping every time we drove over a bump or rough road. Chopper was unused to driving and was meowing especially when looking out the window.

We stopped at the Matanuska Glacier to take in the view.

We drove as far as Glennallen, and found out that the B&B had no vacancy. We stayed at the local hotel that would not accept pets. So Chopper stayed in his cage all night because the hotel would accept service animals only.

Day 2 – Alaska to Canada

We drove off with a cup of complementary coffee – but I used my own paper hot cup. I wrote a polite note to the owner addressing the fact that a hot beverage in a styrofoam cup is a potential health hazard.

The destination was Tok, Alaska, to access the Alaska Highway a/k/a, Alcan. Temperature was in the 40s; cloudy.

After reaching the Canadian border around seven p.m., we decided to stay at Beaver Creek just across the border into the Yukon, Canada's most westerly situated community.

Of note is that the Yukon entered confederation in 1898, after a gold rush boom led Canada to create a second northern territory out of the North-West Territories.

With four options to stay that night, I chose the place where Chopper was welcome. Just looking outside, you could not tell what time of day or night it actually was without looking at a clock.

DAY 3 – THE YUKON

After some morning coffee, Chopper and I left Beaver Creek, continuing on the Alcan - destination Whitehorse.

I didn't want to run the risk of running out of gas so we stopped at Destruction Bay, which I renamed "Destruction Hair" because of the wind. I also bought a refrigerator magnet with a picture of the Alaska Highway on it and wondered, where do I keep this in the meantime to avoid destruction of credit card and flash drives.

We stopped by Kluane Lake to admire the water.

After arriving in Whitehorse, I decided to check out the Visitor Center, where I was able to recharge my phone and get a map. I was hungry for a salad. I wanted to eat something beneficial for my health, especially for eyesight which is essential for a road trip. My road tripping wish list for eye care included zeaxanthin and lutein. My road tripping menu for eye care included a salad of leafy green vegetables for zeaxanthin: kale, spinach, romaine lettuce, watercress, Swiss chard, turnip greens, collard greens, mustard greens. A hard boiled egg, sliced in half, topped the salad - for a source of lutein. My wish list for dessert: spirulina tablets. Beverages: green tea and carrot juice.

When we reached Teslin, I really knew I was in Canada when I saw Nanaimo Bars for sale at the local trading post. Only in Canada – an unpackaged delicacy with chocolate/coconut base and yellow custard filling, topped with chocolate. Too yummy to pass up – so I bought a Nanaimo Bar. My mother used to make them.

We ended up at Watson Lake that night and stayed at a pet-friendly hotel. The bed was on blocks and this time Chopper could not hide under the bed.

DAY 4 – THE YUKON TO BRITISH COLUMBIA

Before leaving Watson Lake, I wanted to make a purchase and found out that pennies were not used in trade. The copper penny was phased out in Canada in 2013. Of note is that the halfpenny in the U.K. was phased out in 1984.

Continuing down the main road of Watson Lake, I was hoping to be on the correct route and was relieved to see the sign "Alaska Highway" alongside the road and then a second sign in French.

Not far was the Yukon/British Columbia border, where two bison were grazing.

We reached Muncho Lake. The scenery was spectacular. The jade green color of the lake was stunning.

Bighorn mountain sheep were along the highway.

13

End of May: Ice melting on Summit Lake.

We drove and stopped for more gas because I didn't want to risk being stranded with an empty tank.

Back on the Alcan, I saw a dark blob in the distance at the side of the road. I was thinking, if you have "big feet" I'm on my way to take your picture! It was a moose.

Several black bears were spotted at the roadside.

Rain: the best thing to clean my windshield considering all the insects that had collided.

When we arrived at Fort Nelson, there was thundering and lightning. Chopper and I stayed at a motel chain where we regrouped for the next day.

Day 5 – End of the Alaska Highway

Because I had received all the tourist info I needed from the chain motel, I did not stop at Fort Nelson's Visitor Center. After filling gas at Petro-Canada, Chopper and I headed south.

We stopped for a photo at Polk A Dot Creek.

Driving has been smooth this whole trip. I saw no potholes except for repaired ones. At times the Alaska Highway was gravel-topped and there had been some road construction.

We continued driving, ending the day at Mile 0 of the Alaska Highway at Dawson Creek. Completed in 1942, the Alaska Highway turns 75 years old this year.

DAY 6 – BRITISH COLUMBIA TO ALBERTA

Our first stop in the morning was to Dawson Creek's Visitor Center, where we received maps of both Alberta and Saskatchewan, courtesy of the Alberta Government.

Chopper and I left the Alaska Highway at the intersection where the Visitor Center was located, heading out to Petro-Canada to fill the tank and order a large medium roast coffee. Soon we'd be crossing the border into Alberta.

I decided to make a detour to visit two nieces in northern Alberta. So after driving through Grand Prairie and Valleyview, Chopper and I headed north toward High Prairie and Slave Lake.

We drove as far as Athabasca, and stopped at a pet-friendly chain motel. (This was a new luxury motel and difficult to leave.) So far there had been no pet accidents. Chopper used his disposable litter boxes that I had made in advance consisting of small pineapple juice boxes lined with 13-gallon trash bags, filled with clay litter.

Day 7 – Fort McMurray AB

Checking out at one p.m., we then filled gas at Petro-Canada before the three-hour drive north to Fort McMurray.

As we drove closer to Fort McMurray, it was apparent there had been a fire there. Just a year ago 88,000 people evacuated the city due to a fire which may have been started by a cigarette tossed from a window. The police suspect careless action as the cause of the fire.

That evening my nieces Amanda and Angela, and Mike (Amanda's fiancé) met at a nice restaurant where we caught up on all the family news.

Day 8 – Fort McMurray AB

Being a tourist is always nicer when your niece can be your tour guide. Amanda, off work today, drove me around Fort McMurray and showed me where the fire had burned down houses, now replaced by new construction.

Later in the evening, my other niece, Angela, stopped by after her day of work as an avian biologist for the oil industry. Angela focuses on bird conservation. While driving around town, we saw bus after bus transporting oil industry workers to and from the jobsite, several shifts a day. We also went to the mall where we enjoyed some New York Fries.

Day 9 – Alberta to Saskatchewan

In the morning Chopper and I left Fort McMurray and backtracked to Athabasca. We followed the road signs to our destination of St. Albert, also known as the Botanical Arts City, to visit my nephew who now has his own acupuncture clinic. We met along the highway in the Costco parking lot and then drove to a local gardening center where we ate and took some pix. Our salads were delicious; all flowers were phenomenal and fragrant; and the weather was warm and sunny. We are in the first week of June, just outside of Edmonton.

Then Chopper and I accessed the Yellowhead Highway heading to Saskatchewan, to visit my sister Leona. She met us ten miles east of North Battleford at the intersection of Highway 40 and the grid road, and I followed her to her farm where she and her husband live.

Chopper had a good time roaming the house and it was good for him to get some exercise after being cooped up all day in his kennel.

The highlight of the day was the RCMP Musical Ride at Fort Battleford, a national historical site. The RCMP (Royal Canadian Mounted Police) is on national tour this year in commemoration of the 150th anniversary of Canadian confederation. The weather cooperated and truly it was a great day.

Day 10 – Fort Battleford SK

Fort Battleford was built in 1876, located at the confluence of the North Saskatchewan and the Battle rivers at Battleford.

The river, like the province of Saskatchewan, takes its name from the Cree word kisiskâciwanisîpiy meaning "swift flowing river". The river, labeled as the Kish-stock-ewen, is identified on a Hudson's Bay Company map of 1760.

Day 10 (Continued) – Battleford SK

Then Leona and I drove to Battleford to see a monument of Government House (1877 - 1883), as Battleford was the newly designated capital of the North-West Territories, an area then comprising over two-thirds of Canada.

The Town of Battleford is directly across the North Saskatchewan River from the City of North Battleford.

Unfortunately the historical Government House was destroyed by fire in 2003.

Day 11 – North Battleford SK

In the morning we decided to indulge in the Lavender Frosty, a non-dairy ice cream recipe from my hard-cover book, *Fire & Ice: ALASKA – Baked, Blended, & Sautéed*, Frosty Books (2012), www.frostybooks.com; info@frostybooks.com.

<u>Lavender Frosty</u>

    1-1/4 tsp dried lavender flowers
    1/2 c water
    3/4 c almonds
    1/4 tsp flax seed
    1/2 tsp liquid lecithin
    1 tsp liquid honey
    2 c frozen blueberries

Heat water in small saucepan to near boiling; remove from heat and add dried lavender flowers; steep x 10 minutes. Transfer to fridge to cool x 10 minutes.

Add all ingredients except frozen blueberries to "power" blender (I use a Vita Mix) and liquefy on high speed. Add frozen blueberries and combine on medium speed until smooth. Serve immediately in chilled glass or bowl. Yields 1 pint.

Liquid lecithin, which is also classified as a "health food" is used as an emulsifier in this recipe. I was happy that Leona had this ingredient on hand, which she had purchased from a natural foods store in North Battleford. She says she uses it all the time to prepare the Chocolate Frosty recipe. I purchased liquid lecithin in pint bottles at a natural foods store in Anchorage. Liquid lecithin is also available for sale online.

DAY 11 (CONTINUED) – DAVIN SK

After raving over the Lavender Frosty, I packed the SUV ready to go, except for Chopper who was hiding out. A quick search of the house revealed the cat hiding under the pink chair in the basement. Apparently Chopper did not want to leave the farm at North Battleford.

Leona and her husband David had appointments in Saskatoon, so Chopper and I followed their car to the main highway. We filled gas in Saskatoon, and headed south to the hamlet of Davin, southeast of Regina twenty plus miles away where I completed grade VIII (alum '70) at Davin School (1910 – 1973).

It was spraying season on the family farm c/o Albert (one of the twins).

Albert and Edward Leippi with twelve hundred-gallon tank, filled with water from their creek.

Overflowing creek one mile south of the farmyard. Rural Municipality of Lajord.

We checked out a copy of the original land title from 1899. The land had been purchased from the country by my great-grandfather and it was interesting to note that "Assiniboia, Canada" was recorded on the title.

In 1882, four districts were formed: Alberta, Athabasca, Assiniboia, and Saskatchewan. Saskatchewan became a province in 1905, and so did Alberta.

While in Davin, I visited two brothers, Edward and Albert, who farm the family farm. I also stopped by to visit cousins David & Sheila Brandt, who farm the Brandt family farm.

DAY 12 – REGINA SK

Today I drove to Regina, the province's capital, without Chopper and without the box of cat toys that sounded off every time I hit a bump in the road.

Destination: Government House, built in 1891, that served as the official residence and office of the Lieutenant Governor of the North-West Territories. Present day Government House is a multi-purpose Heritage Facility as well as the working office of the Lieutenant Governor (the Queen's representative of Saskatchewan).

I stayed for a children's program held in the ballroom followed by a reception, and had the opportunity to see and hear the lieutenant governor speak before a local author gave a presentation to a group of school children.

Enjoying a bowl of delicious beet soup with Peg and Vern Leippi at Peg's Kitchen, on Park Street in Regina.

The Canadian Pacific Railway was incorporated in 1881 and completed in 1885, and passes through Regina. Regina was founded in 1882. In 1883, Regina was the newly designated capital of the North-West Territories, until 1905. Regina has been the capital of Saskatchewan since 1905.

The Latin word for "queen" is "Regina". The British monarchy named the town (at that time it was a town) "Regina". The name "Victoria" was already taken as a capital, as British Columbia had joined confederation in 1871, becoming Canada's sixth province. The British pronunciation for Regina is "rej eye nuh".

While in Regina, I stopped by a friend Patricia Holdsworth's place for a cup of tea. Several years earlier she had done food photography for the Fire & Ice cookbook. Today I gave her a glass mug of dried lavender flowers as I had been giving all friends and relatives who have a copy of the Fire & Ice cookbook.

On returning to Davin that evening, I stopped by a friend and neighbor Donna Klein's house and talked with her and her husband Merv for several hours about what was happening around town.

Day 13 – Regina SK

Back to Regina today, this time to visit the RCMP Heritage Center. This is also the location for the training depot for all RCMP recruits. I was there by noon for a tour which included a parade and a tour of the chapel, the oldest standing building in Regina today, built in 1885 as a mess hall and then turned into a chapel in 1895. The museum was filled with historical artifacts dating back to 1873, when the RCMP was established as the North-West Mounted Police. A movie was shown.

In between the RCMP barracks and Government House is Luther College where I had attended high school (alum '74). I stopped by to donate a signed Fire & Ice cookbook for their library.

Down the street from Luther College on Dewdney Avenue is the old courthouse, a historical building with a monument. In 1885, Louis Riel was hanged there following two resistance movements.

After refueling and returning to Davin, I visited with aunt Elsie and uncle Ron (82-y-o & 84-y-o) married sixty years now. They shared pictures of their children, grandchildren, and great-grandchildren.

I returned to the home of one of my brothers, and Chopper and I visited with both of them before calling a day a day.

DAY 14 – SASKATCHEWAN TO MANITOBA

I left Davin with Chopper and drove through Fort Qu'Appelle and Melville, stopping at Yorkton to refuel.

Destination: Pelly, Saskatchewan, a former Hudson's Bay trading post, in search of Fort Livingstone, the newly designated capital of the North-West Territories (1876 – 1877). Unfortunately Fort Livingstone had burned down and so did the museum.

Fort Livingstone was built in 1874, for the newly-formed North-West Mounted Police. The location was chosen by the federal government as a temporary site to establish the new territorial government until the route of the railway was determined. It served as the temporary seat of government of the North-West Territories while the new government buildings in Battleford were being constructed.

At the close of day, Chopper and I reached Dauphin, Manitoba, where we stopped at a pet-friendly hotel.

DAY 15 – MANITOBA

Chopper and I left Dauphin and eventually arrived at Riding Mountain National Park of Canada. Admission was free for 2017, to help celebrate Canada turning 150 on July 1st.

While on pavement we drove slowly with all four windows down, breathing in the fresh air and admiring the scenery, on alert to spot any wildlife. The scenery (trees and lakes) was breathtaking. We exited the park through the historical east gate, the only original park entrance in Canada.

We continued to Winnipeg, and I couldn't resist finishing the day with a bowl of delicious beet soup served by Dani.

Day 16 – Manitoba to Ontario

We got off to a late start due to lack of sleep the night before at a pet-friendly motel chain (a senior citizen's loud TV in next room). Looking back, I can say that I learned tolerance!

In spite of a late check-out, we arrived at Lower Fort Garry right on time for an orientation and a tour of the fort dating back to 1830. Located north of Winnipeg, the fort was a page out of history.

Tour guide Dustin took our group to the Red River which flows north into Lake Winnipeg.

Several ox carts were on display.

The blacksmith shop was interesting, especially the wooden frame in front of the blacksmith shop where oxen were hoisted up to be shoed, as oxen cannot balance on their own while being shoed. Each oxshoe has two parts because of the cloven hoof.

The Hudson's Bay Company from London, England, established in 1670, had headquarters at Fort Garry.

The Rupert's Land Act 1868, enacted by the Parliament of the United Kingdom, resulted in the remaining territory as the North-West Territories and was brought under Canadian jurisdiction.

In 1869/1870 the transfer of the North-West Territories from the Hudson's Bay Company to the Dominion of Canada became a major point of contention. Manitoba became a province in 1870. Winnipeg, the capital of Manitoba, was established in 1873.

The NWT capital was transferred west from Lower Fort Garry to Fort Livingstone at Pelly, Saskatchewan (1876 – 1877). The current capital of the North-West Territories is Yellowknife.

After leaving the fort we drove as far as Kenora, Ontario, and stayed at a pet-friendly motel chain where we saw two black bears behind the motel. In the motel room, the drapes didn't close one hundred percent but fortunately I had a plastic bag-closing clip in my SUV, and so I used the plastic clip to close the drapes.

DAY 17 – ONTARIO

Leaving Kenora in the a.m. we drove past lovely lakes and trees.

At Dryden, we stopped at a wand carwash and I changed out some Canadian dollar bills for coin. I'm glad I didn't leave Alaska without microfiber cloths – always great for a road trip because one never knows when they will come in handy, especially when traveling with a pet.

As a dual citizen I started out the journey with both U.S. and Canadian cash. Most places accepted my credit card; one place would not. Generally speaking credit card transactions were easy, and showed up on my statement in Canadian funds.

Since the road trip, I opened a TD Bank account that offers free access at TD ATMs in the U.S. and Canada.

We passed by Thunder Bay and drove until Nipigon, where we found a pet-friendly motel.

Day 18 – Ontario

That morning in Nipigon, I stopped at the Visitor Center for a map of Ontario, courtesy of the Government of Ontario.

Chopper and I headed east, adding gas at Wawa, then driving past Lake Superior. What an amazing view of the water!

We drove as far as Sault Ste. Marie (soo saint marie). Looking at the map I was wondering why more miles weren't covered, but there had been a lot of road construction.

Anything worse than road construction? Toll roads possibly.

Day 19 – Ontario

Chopper was hiding under the bed when it was time to leave our pet-friendly motel in Sault Ste. Marie. Just a swipe under the bed with the handle of my long-handled gold panning spade, that doubles in winter as a tiny snow shovel, was enough to make him surface.

After several hours I stopped at a fast food chain to buy some cold fruit juice as well as use the restroom. I noted that the best bathrooms are at fast food restaurants and visitor centers.

Usually better than gas stations although there's always exceptions. Much better than outhouses along the highway, and always better than squatting by a tree. Driving with a full bladder – not good.

We reached Deep River, and stayed at a pet-friendly motel. In the bathroom I noticed a plastic shower curtain which is a potential health hazard, and politely asked if the plastic shower curtain could be changed out for a fabric one. Within the hour I had a fabric shower curtain.

After the road trip, I did decline to stay in a motel that would not change out a plastic shower curtain.

DAY 20 – CANADA TO U.S.A.

This morning Chopper was adventurous and traveled into the box spring mattress. The motel owner helped tip the mattress, and Chopper emerged. We left Deep River after receiving a map of Ottawa from the motel owner, and directions to Parliament Hill just two hours away.

We parked in the parking garage at the World Exchange Plaza just a few blocks from Parliament Hill. Tourists were everywhere. I bought a red T-shirt from a souvenir shop. The weather was perfect: warm and sunny.

This was my first drive to Ottawa, the nation's capital. I felt this was a good year to visit as 2017 marks the 150th anniversary of Canada, or the 150th anniversary of Confederation (1867 – 2017) when Canada became self-governing, under the British Empire. Canada's initial provinces at confederation were Ontario, New Brunswick, Québec, and Nova Scotia.

I was happy to join a group tour of the Supreme Court of Canada, hosted by Sophie. All tours were free and were first come, first serve.

Prince Edward Island (PEI) joined confederation in 1873. Newfoundland and Labrador joined confederation in 1949. Nunavut was carved out of the North-West Territories in 1999.

Before returning to the parking garage, I explored the food court at the World Exchange Plaza and found Nanaimo bars and of course bought the tasty treat.

The attendant in the parking garage gave directions on how to exit Ottawa, and so we headed south to the U.S. border. My Canadian auto insurance coverage expired at midnight.

The drive over the Ogdensburg–Prescott International Bridge, connecting Johnstown, Ontario and Ogdensburg, New York, took us from Canada to the United States. Chopper and I drove one and a half miles on the suspension bridge across the Saint Lawrence River and Saint Lawrence Seaway.

When we reached New York State, our destination seemed closer than ever. After stopping for the night, I realized that we were able to locate pet-friendly accommodations for all nights except for our first night on the road.

DAY 21 – ARRIVING IN NEW YORK CITY

Our final day on the road, as usual I tried to keep a steady foot on the accelerator for better gas mileage. Stopping to wash the Ford Explorer one more time, our journey took us all the way to New York City, arriving at our destination and parking the SUV in the parking garage.

Driving with GPS on my iPhone was extremely useful and when the charge died, I switched over to the GPS on the iPad tablet.

The chargers stayed plugged into the devices and were not misplaced.

Chopper and I arrived in Williamsburg in Brooklyn in rush hour traffic that evening. Three weeks and fifty-six hundred miles later, here we are. Without good weather and the GPS, driving would have been difficult.

We made it!

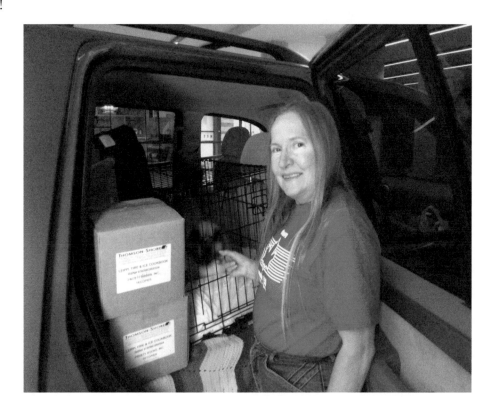

Printed in the United States
By Bookmasters